MARUTHI KRISHNA'S SPELLING –1:

4100 SPELLINGS

MARUTHI KRISHNA NIVARTHI

M.A.(English), (Ph.D.), B.Ed.

Assistant Professor

DEDICATION

This book is dedicated to my parents.

CONTENTS

ACKNOWLEDGMENTS

The following sources have been used in writing this book.

1.Oxford Advanced Learner's Dictionary
2.Cambridge Dictionary
3.Collins Dictionary
4.Merriam-Webster Dictionary

1.Introduction

In this book, whose title is Maruthi Krishna's Spelling-1, the spellings of nearly 4100 words are written   in their alphabetical order. These spellings can be learnt by   a student preparing for spelling competitions or trying to get a very good command on spellings following the division of these spellings into sets of 30 words each. Of course, based on the need and the speed of the learning, he/she can learn two days' spellings in a single day, or a teacher can guide the students to do so.

In this book, most of the important nouns, verbs, adjectives and adverbs are given. The names of the days, the months, the planets, continents and almost all the animals are also included in this book. Care has been taken to include all the important spellings from Physics, Chemistry, Maths, Biology, Social, etc. subjects.

In the second book, whose title is Maruthi Krishna's Spellings-2, which will be released in a month or so, the remaining important nouns, adjectives, verbs, adverbs, the names of all the countries, the important cities in the world, the names of the states, the currencies, etc. are written.

Before starting to learn spellings for competitions, a student has to learn the rules and the regular practices and the differences between the spellings of the British and the American varieties of English. So, they are given in the next chapter.

The educational institutions which want to improve the performance of their students in reciting and writing spellings can make use of this book by making the students download this book and learn the spellings as per the division given in this book and taking the help of the English teachers. The division has been done keeping in mind that the learning of spellings should not interfere with the learning of question and answers or doing of the homework of the subjects of the students. The students should be made learn the twenty-five spellings of a day only after he or she has done the homework from the subjects for the day. This book can be introduced in the 8th or the 9th standard, and the English teachers can ask any five students randomly the next day to recite the spellings after a day's spellings are learnt by them. Of course, they can conduct a simple dictation in the first five minutes of their class every day. The English teachers can repeat this process until all the spellings in this book are learnt. At the end of the students' learning of all the spellings, they can conduct a "Spell Bee" competition at the class or the school level and appreciate the winner and the runner-up.

2. Rules of Spellings

1.Generally, no letter is removed from a verb

   when the suffix -**ment** is added to it to

   write its noun.   Look at the following

   examples.

   Improve--Improve**ment**

   Entertain--Entertain**ment**

   Treat--Treat**ment**

   Commit--Commit**ment**

2.Generally, 'y' at the end of a word is
   replaced with 'i' before **-ness, -ment, or -
   ance** is added to it. Look at the following
   examples.

   Happ**y**--Happ**iness**

   Laz**y**--Laz**iness**

   Sleep**y**--Sleep**iness**

   Rel**y**--Rel**iance**

   Merr**y**--Merr**iment**

3. Generally, the letter 'e' at the end of a
   word is removed before **-ing** is added
   to it. Look at the following examples.

Create- -Creating

Accuse--Accusing

Write--Writing

Remove--Removing

4. Generally, when a word ends with 'al', no letter is added or removed before _-ity_ is added to it. Look at the following examples.

Practical--Practicality

Partial--Partiality

Equal--Equality

Local--Locality

Total--Totality
Vital--Vitality

Trivial--Triviality

5. Generally, when the name of a study ends with 'gy', to mention the person who studies it, the spelling _-ist_ is added after the letter 'y' is removed. Look at the following examples.

Urology—Urologist

Anthropology—Anthropologist

Psychology—Psychologist

Nephrology—Nephrologist

Cardiology—Cardiologist

Ornithology--Ornithologist

6. Generally, when a word ends with 'phy', the letter 'y' is removed before 'er' is added to it. Look at the following examples.

Biography—Biographer

Calligraphy—Calligrapher

Auto-biography--Auto-biographer

Cartography—Cartographer

7. Generally, if a word ends with 'ic', no letter is added or removed before -ian is added to it. Look at the following examples.

Music—Musicial

Magic—Magician

Electric --Electrician

Phonetic—Phonetician

8.Generally, in the adjectives that end with 'y', in the formation of their comparative and superlative degrees, that 'y' is replaced with 'i' before 'er' or 'est' is added to that adjective. Look at the following examples.

Happy --Happier

Merry—Merrier
Busy—Busier

Wealthy--Wealthier

Happy--Happiest

Merry--Merriest

Busy--Busiest

Wealthy--Wealthiest

9.Generally, when an adjective ends with 'e', in the formation of its comparative and superlative degrees, 'r' or 'st' is added without adding or removing any letter. Look at the following examples.

Safe—Safer

White—Whiter

Safe—Safest

White*e*—Whit*est*

10.Generally, 'ble' at the end of a word is replaced with 'bil' before '-ity' is added to it. Look at the following examples.

Capa*ble*—Capa*bility*

Visi*ble*—Visi*bility*

Feasi*ble*—Feasi*bility*

Credi*ble*—Credi*bility*

3. The British and the American Varieties

1. In many words, the ending 'our' in the British variety is replaced with 'or' in the American variety. Look at the following examples.

Flav<u>our</u> (BrE)---Flav<u>or</u> (AmE)

Neighb<u>our</u> (BrE)---Neighb<u>or</u> (AmE)

Behavi<u>our</u> (BrE)---Behavi<u>or</u> (AmE)

Fav<u>our</u> (BrE)---Fav<u>or</u> (AmE)

Col<u>our</u> (BrE)---Col<u>or</u> (AmE)

Endeav<u>our</u> (BrE)---Endeav<u>or</u> (AmE)

2. In many words, the ending 're' in the British variety is replaced with 'er' in the American variety. Look at the following examples.

Cent<u>re</u> (BrE)---Cent<u>er</u> (AmE)

Lit<u>re</u> (BrE)---Lit<u>er</u> (AmE)

3. In many words, the ending 'se' in the British variety is replaced with 'ze' in the American variety. Look at the following

examples.

> Emphasi<u>se</u> (BrE)---Emphasi<u>ze</u> (AmE)
>
> Organi<u>se</u> (BrE)---Organi<u>ze</u> (AmE)
>
> Speciali<u>sed</u> (BrE)---Speciali<u>zed</u> (AmE)
>
> Sterili<u>se</u> (BrE)---Sterili<u>ze</u> (AmE)
>
> Recogni<u>se</u> (BrE)---Recogni<u>ze</u> (AmE)

4.In many words, the British 'paed' spelling is replaced with ''ped' in the American variety.

> Ortho<u>pae</u>dic (BrE)---Ortho<u>pe</u>dic (AmE)
>
> <u>Pae</u>diatrician (BrE)---<u>Pe</u>diatrician (AmE)
>
> Encyclo<u>pae</u>dia (BrE)---Encyclo<u>pe</u>dia (AmE)

4. Spellings

Day-1

1. Abdomen

2. Abnormal

3. Abrupt

4. Abruptly

5. Absence

6. Absent

7. Absentee

8. Abstract

9. Abundant

10. Abusive

11. Academician

12. Acceleration

13. Accept

14. Acceptor

15. Accident

16. Accidental

17. Accommodation

18. Accomplice

19. Accordance

20. Accountant

21. Accredit

22. Accreditation

23. Accusation

24. Accuse

25. Acidic

26. Acknowledge

27. Acoustic

28. Acquit

29. Acquittal

30. Across

Day-2

31. Activist

32. Actor

33. Ad

34. Adamant

35. Adapt

36. Addition

37. Address

38. Addressee

39. Addressee

40. Addresser

41. Adept

42. Adhere

43. Adjective

44. Adjourn

45. Adjustment

46. Administration

47. Administrator

48. Admission

49. Admittance

50. Admonish

51. Adolescence

52. Adolescent

53. Adopt

54. Adult

55. Advantage

56. Adventure

57. Adventurer

58. Adventurous

59. Adverb

60. Advertisement

Day-3

61. Advertiser

62. Advice

63. Advise

64. Adviser/advisor

65. Advocate

66. Aerobic

67. Aerodrome

68. Aeroplane

69. Affairs

70. Affect

71. Affectionate

72. Affix

73. Afraid

74. Afro-American

75. Afternoon

76. Aggravate

77. Aggregate

78. Agitator

79. Agnostic

80. Agree

81. Agreement

82. Agricultural

83. Agriculture

84. Aid

85. Ail

86. Ailment

87. Air conditioner

88. Aisle

89. Alarm

90. Albatross

Day-4

91. Ale

92. Alert

93. Algebra

94. Alien

95. Alike

96. Alkaline

97. All

98. All right

99. Allay

100. Allegation

101. Allegedly

102. Alligator

103. Allophone

104. Allot

105. Allow

106. Allowance

107. Allure

108. Allusion

109. Alluvial

110. Ally

111. Almirah

112. Almond

113. Almost

114. Alms

115. Alone

116. Alright

117. Altar

118. Alter

119. Alternate

120. Alternative

Day-5

121. Alternatively

122. Alum

123. Aluminium

124. Amazon

125. Ambidextrous

126. Ambition

127. Ambitious

128. Ambivalent

129. Amendment

130. Amethyst

131. Amiable

132. Amicable

133. Amicably

134. Amid

135. Amidst

136. Amoeba

137. Amount

138. Ampere

139. Amphibian

140. Amputate

141. Amuse

142. Anagram

143. Analyse (BrE) / Analyze (USA)

144. Analysis

145. Anarchy

146. Anathema

147. Anatomy

148. Ancestor

149. Anchor

150. Anchors

Day-6

151. Ancient

152. Ankle

153. Annotate

154. Announce

155. Annum

156. Answer

157. Antelope

158. Antenna

159. Anthem

160. Anthropologist

161. Antibiotic

162. Anti-septic

163. Antler

164. Apart

165. Apartment

166. Apathy

167. Apex

168. Aphelion

169. Appalling

170. Apparent

171. Apparently

172. Appeal

173. Appear

174. Appetite

175. Applaud

176. Applicant

177. Application

178. Appoint

179. Appointee

180. Apposite

Day-7

181. Appreciate

182. Approve

183. Approver

184. April

185. Aquarium

186. Aquatic

187. Arabian

188. Arc

189. Arch

190. Archaeologist

191. Archaeology

192. Architect

193. Architecture

194. Arctic

195. Area

196. Argumentative

197. Arise

198. Arisen

199. Aristocracy

200. Aristocratic

201. Ark

202. Armadillo

203. Arose

204. Array

205. Arrears

206. Arrive

207. Arrogant

208. Arrow

209. Artery

210. Artful

Day-8

211. Article

212. Artist

213. Artiste

214. Ascend

215. Asian

216. Assassin

217. Assay

218. Assemble

219. Assembly

220. Assent

221. Assertive

222. Assess

223. Assessor

224. Asset

225. Assistant

226. Associate

227. Association

228. Assume

229. Assumption

230. Assurance

231. Assure

232. Astrologer

233. Astrology

234. Astronomer

235. Astronomy

236. Atheist

237. Athlete

238. Atlantic

239. Atmosphere

240. Attack

Day-9

241. Attain

242. Attainment

243. Attendance

244. Attendee

245. Attitude

246. Auctioneer

247. Audible

248. Audience

249. Auditor

250. Auditorium

251. August

252. Aunt

253. Aural

254. Austrian

255. Author

256. Authoress

257. Authorship

258. Auto-biographer

259. Autobiography

260. Automatic

261. Autonomous

262. Autonomy

263. Autumn

264. Availability

265. Avenge

266. Avenger

267. Avenue

268. Aversion

269. Avid

270. Avocado

Day-10

271. Avoid

272. Award

273. Awareness

274. Awful

275. Awkward

276. Awl

277. Axe

278. Babble

279. Baboon

280. Baby

281. Bacteria

282. Badger

283. Badminton

284. Baggage

285. Baize

286. Bake

287. Baked

288. Bakery

289. Bald

290. Bale

291. Balm

292. Ban

293. Bandage

294. Bandwagon

295. Bane

296. Bankrupt

297. Bankruptcy

298. Banned

299. Barbarous

300. Bard

Day-11

301. Bare

302. Baron

303. Barred

304. Barren

305. Basilisk

306. Bat

307. Bath

308. Bathe

309. Batsman

310. Batter

311. Bauxite

312. Bawled

313. Bay of Bengal

314. Bays

315. Beach

316. Beagle

317. Bean

318. Bear

319. Beatboxer

320. Beautician

321. Beautiful

322. Beautifully

323. Beauty

324. Beaver

325. Beckon

326. Bedding

327. Bee

328. Beech

329. Been

330. Beer

Day-12

331. Behaviour

332. Belch

333. Belief

334. Believe

335. Believer

336. Beneath

337. Benedict

338. Benediction

339. Benefaction

340. Benefactor

341. Beneficence

342. Beneficent

343. Beneficial

344. Beneficiaries

345. Beneficiary

346. Benevolence

347. Benevolent

348. Benign

349. Benzene

350. Beri-Beri

351. Berry

352. Berth

353. Betray

354. Betrayal

355. Beverage

356. Biannual

357. Biased

358. Bible

359. Bibliophile

360. Bicycle

Day-13

361. Bier

362. Biker

363. Billiards

364. Billion

365. Billionaire

366. Binary

367. Binoculars

368. Biodegradable

369. Biographer

370. Biography

371. Bird

372. Birth

373. Biscuit

374. Bishop

375. Bison

376. Bitter

377. Black

378. Blade

379. Bled

380. Bleed

381. Block

382. Blogger

383. Blood

384. Board

385. Boil

386. Bold

387. Bona fide

388. Bookie

389. Boomerang

390. Boon

Day-14

391. Boredom

392. Boring

393. Born

394. Borne

395. Borrow

396. Borrower

397. Bottle

398. Bough

399. Boulder

400. Bounce

401. Bouncer

402. Bowl

403. Bowler

404. Boxing

405. Braid

406. Brain

407. Brake

408. Branch

409. Brass

410. Brave

411. Bravery

412. Bray

413. Breach

414. Bread

415. Breadth

416. Break

417. Breakfast

418. Breath

419. Breathe

420. Breathed

Day-15

421. Breeze

422. Brevity

423. Brew

424. Bridal

425. Bride

426. Bridegroom

427. Bridle

428. Brigadier

429. Brilliant

430. Brinjal

431. Bristle

432. Britons

433. Brittle

434. Broad

435. Broadcaster

436. Broccoli

437. Broker

438. Brotherhood

439. Brother-in-law

440. Bruise

441. Brunch

442. Brunette

443. Bubble

444. Buffalo

445. Buffaloes

446. Build

447. Builder

448. Built

449. Bull

450. Bullock

Day-16

451. Bun

452. Bureau

453. Bureaucracy

454. Bureaucrat

455. Burger

456. Burglar

457. Burial

458. Burn

459. Burnt

460. Burrow

461. Bury

462. Bus stand

463. Butler

464. Buy

465. Buyer

466. Bypass

467. Cab

468. Cache

469. Cactus

470. Cake

471. Calamity

472. Calculate

473. Calculator

474. Calculus

475. Calendar

476. Calender

477. Calf

478. Calligrapher

479. Calligraphy

480. Calves

Day-17

481. Camel

482. Camera

483. Campaign

484. Campaigner

485. Canal

486. Cancer

487. Candidate

488. Candidature

489. Candle

490. Candy

491. Cannibal

492. Cannon

493. Canon

494. Canopy

495. Canvas

496. Canvass

497. Capability

498. Capable

499. Capacity

500. Capital

501. Capitol

502. Capsicum

503. Captain

504. Carbon

505. Carbon Monoxide

506. Carbonated

507. Cardamom

508. Cardinal

509. Cardiology

510. Cardiologist

Day-18

511. Cardiovascular

512. Career

513. Carnivore

514. Carnivorous

515. Carpenter

516. Carrier

517. Carry

518. Cart

519. Cartographer

520. Cartoonist

521. Cash

522. Cashew

523. Caspian

524. Cassette

525. Cast

526. Caste

527. Castle

528. Castor oil

529. Casual

530. Casually

531. Cater

532. Cathedral

533. Catholic

534. Cause

535. Caustic

536. Cavernous

537. Ceiling

538. Celestial

539. Celsius

540. Cenotaph

Day-19

541. Censer

542. Censor

543. Censure

544. Cent

545. Centenarian

546. Centipede

547. Centre (UK) / Center (USA)

548. Centrifugal

549. Century

550. Ceremonious

551. Ceremony

552. Certain

553. Certainly

554. Certainty

555. Chain

556. Chair

557. Chalk

558. Challenge

559. Chamber

560. Chameleon

561. Champagne

562. Champion

563. Chancellor

564. Chandelier

565. Channel

566. Chaos

567. Chapel

568. Chappal

569. Character

570. Characteristic

Day-20

571. Charcoal

572. Chariot

573. Charisma

574. Charitable

575. Charity

576. Charter

577. Chartered Accountant

578. Chase

579. Chaste

580. Chastity

581. Chat

582. Chatter

583. Cheap

584. Check

585. Checkmate

586. Cheer

587. Cheetah

588. Chef

589. Chemical

590. Chemist

591. Chemistry

592. Cheque

593. Cherish

594. Chess

595. Chew

596. Chicken

597. Chief

598. Child

599. Childhood

600.   Childish

Day-21

601. Children

602. Chill

603. Chimpanzee

604. Chinese

605. Chirp

606. Chocolate

607. Choice

608. Choir

609. Cholesterol

610. Choose

611. Choral

612. Choreographer

613. Chorus

614. Chose

615. Chosen

616. Chronological

617. Chronology

618. Chunk

619. Church

620. Cigar

621. Cigarette

622. Circular

623. Circulate

624. Circumference

625. Cite

626. Citizen

627. Citrus

628. Civics

629. Civilian

630. Claim

Day-22

631. Claimant

632. Clan

633. Clang

634. Clap

635. Clapped

636. Classify

637. Clause

638. Claustrophobia

639. Clay

640. Clever

641. Cleverly

642. Cleverness

643. Click

644. Client

645. Cliff

646. Clock

647. Clove

648. Clover

649. Cloves

650. Clown

651. Club

652. Coach

653. Coarse

654. Co-author

655. Cobbler

656. Cobra

657. Coconut

658. Code

659. Coffee

660. Cognitive

Day-23

661. Coil

662. Collaborate

663. Collaboration

664. Collapse

665. Collar

666. Collector

667. College

668. Collide

669. Collision

670. Collusion

671. Colonel

672. Colossus

673. Colour (UK) / Color (USA)

674. Column

675. Columnist

676. Combat

677. Comfort

678. Comfortable

679. Command

680. Commendable

681. Comment

682. Commerce

683. Commit

684. Committed

685. Common

686. Commoner

687. Communication

688. Communist

689. Community

690. Compact disc

Day-24

691. Comparison

692. Compass

693. Compel

694. Compelling

695. Competition

696. Competitor

697. Complainant

698. Complaint

699. Complement

700. Complex

701. Compliment

702. Composer

703. Compound

704. Comprise

705. Comptroller

706. Compulsory

707. Computer

708. Conceive

709. Concession

710. Concise

711. Concrete

712. Concreteness

713. Condemn

714. Condensation

715. Condition

716. Condonation

717. Conductor

718. Confer

719. Conferred

720. Confessor

Day-25

721. Confidant

722. Confident

723. Conical

724. Conjunction

725. Connotate

726. Conquer

727. Conqueror

728. Cons

729. Conscience

730. Conscious

731. Consecrate

732. Consecutive

733. Consensus

734. Consequences

735. Consequently

736. Conservation

737. Conservative

738. Consist

739. Consistent

740. Constant

741. Constipation

742. Constitution

743. Constitutional

744. Construct

745. Construction

746. Construe

747. Consume

748. Consumption

749. Contact

750. Contagious

Day-26

751. Contain

752. Container

753. Contemporary

754. Continent

755. Contingent

756. Continuity

757. Continuous

758. Continuously

759. Continuum

760. Contract

761. Contractor

762. Contradictory

763. Contrary

764. Controller

765. Controversial

766. Controversy

767. Convener

768. Convergent

769. Conversion

770. Convert

771. Convey

772. Conveyance

773. Convince

774. Convoluted

775. Cook

776. Cooked

777. Cookie

778. Co-operative

779. Cop

780. Cope

Day-27

781. Copper

782. Cord

783. Coriander

784. Cork

785. Corn

786. Corporal

787. Correct

788. Corrigendum

789. Cosmetics

790. Costumer

791. Cough

792. Council

793. Counsel

794. Counsellor

795. Counterfeit

796. Counterpart

797. Countless

798. Countries

799. Country

800. Couplet

801. Course

802. Cousin

803. Coverage

804. Covid

805. Crab

806. Crack

807. Cradle

808. Crane

809. Crater

810. Crayon

Day-28

811. Creative

812. Creativity

813. Creator

814. Credible

815. Credit

816. Creditable

817. Credulous

818. Cremation

819. Crescent

820. Cricket

821. Cricketer

822. Criminal

823. Criminologist

824. Criminology

825. Crises

826. Crisis

827. Criteria

828. Criterion

829. Crocodile

830. Crooked

831. Crow

832. Crowbar

833. Crowd

834. Crucial

835. Cruelty

836. Crusade

837. Crusader

838. Crux

839. Cryogenics

840. Crystal

Day-29

841. Crystallise (UK) / Crystallize (USA)

842. Cube

843. Cubic

844. Cubicle

845. Cuckoo

846. Cucumber

847. Cue

848. Culprit

849. Cult

850. Culture

851. Cumulative

852. Cunning

853. Cupboard

854. Curator

855. Cure

856. Curfew

857. Curiosity

858. Curious

859. Current

860. Currency

861. Curricula vitae

862. Curriculum

863. Curriculum vitae

864. Curry

865. Curse

866. Curve

867. Cusec

868. Custard apple

869. Customer

870. Cutting

Day-30

871. Cutlery

872. Cyclist

873. Cyclone

874. Dagger

875. Dairy

876. Dais

877. Damp

878. Dampen

879. Dangerous

880. Database

881. Datum

882. Daughter

883. Dawn

884. Daydream

885. Dealer

886. Dear

887. Death

888. Debate

889. Debater

890. Debit

891. Debris

892. Debt

893. Debtor

894. Debut

895. Deceased

896. Deceive

897. December

898. Decency

899. Decent

900. Decibel

Day-31

901. Decimal

902. Decisive

903. Declaration

904. Decoration

905. Decouple

906. Decuple

907. Deduction

908. Deem

909. Deer

910. Defame

911. Defect

912. Defective

913. Defector

914. Defence (UK) / Defense (USA)

915. Defer

916. Deference

917. Deferred

918. Defied

919. Defunct

920. Defy

921. Degrade

922. Degree

923. Deity

924. Delay

925. Delegate

926. Deliberate

927. Deliberately

928. Deliberation

929. Delicacy

930. Delicious

Day-32

931. Delight

932. Delivered

933. Deliverer

934. Delivery

935. Demand

936. Demeanour (UK) / Demeanor (USA)

937. Demigod

938. Demo

939. Democracy

940. Democratic

941. Demographer

942. Demonetisation

943. Demonstration

944. Dengue

945. Denied

946. Denote

947. Dense

948. Density

949. Dental

950. Dentist

951. Dentistry

952. Deny

953. Deodorant

954. Depart

955. Department

956. Dependence

957. Dependent

958. Depict

959. Deposit

960. Depositor

Day-33

961. Depositors

962. Depress

963. Depression

964. Deprivation

965. Derivative

966. Dermatologist

967. Dermatology

968. Derogatory

969. Descend

970. Descent

971. Description

972. Descriptive

973. Desecrate

974. Desecration

975. Desert

976. Design

977. Designate

978. Designation

979. Designer

980. Desire

981. Dessert

982. Destination

983. Destiny

984. Destitute

985. Destroy

986. Detective

987. Detergent

988. Develop

989. Development

990. Develops

Day-34

991. Device

992. Devise

993. Devotee

994. Devout

995. Dew

996. Dexterous

997. Diabetes

998. Diabetic

999. Dial

1000. Dialect

1001. Dialling (UK) / Dialing (USA)

1002. Diamond

1003. Diarist

1004. Diary

1005. Die

1006. Diesel

1007. Differ

1008. Difference

1009. Digger

1010. Dignitaries

1011. Dignitary

1012. Dignity

1013. Dilapidated

1014. Dilemma

1015. Diligent

1016. Dinosaur

1017. Diplomat

1018. Director

1019. Dirt

1020. Dirty

Day-35

1021. Disabled

1022. Disadvantage

1023. Disagree

1024. Disappear

1025. Disaster

1026. Disastrous

1027. Disburse

1028. Discard

1029. Discern

1030. Disciple

1031. Discount

1032. Discourage

1033. Discover

1034. Discoverer

1035. Discovery

1036. Discreet

1037. Discrete

1038. Discretion

1039. Discrimination

1040. Discuss

1041. Discussion

1042. Disease

1043. Disfigure

1044. Dismantle

1045. Dismay

1046. Dismiss

1047. Dismissal

1048. Displacement

1049. Disposal

1050. Disposition

Day-36

1051. Dissent

1052. Dissenter

1053. Dissuade

1054. Distance

1055. Distillation

1056. Distinguished

1057. Distort

1058. Distortion

1059. Distribution

1060. Diurnal

1061. Divergent

1062. Divide

1063. Dividend

1064. Division

1065. Divorce

1066. Divorcee

1067. Dizzy

1068. Doctor

1069. Doctoral

1070. Doctorate

1071. Document

1072. Documentary

1073. Dodo

1074. Does

1075. Doldrums

1076. Dole

1077. Dollar

1078. Dolphin

1079. Dome

1080. Dominant

Day-37

1081. Domination

1082. Don

1083. Donkey

1084. Donor

1085. Doppel ganger

1086. Dormant

1087. Dormitory

1088. Dose

1089. Doubled

1090. Doubtful

1091. Dove

1092. Doze

1093. Dozen

1094. Draft

1095. Drafter

1096. Dragon

1097. Dragonfly

1098. Drainage

1099. Dramatist

1100. Drape

1101. Drastic

1102. Drastically

1103. Draught

1104. Dread

1105. Dreadful

1106. Drinker

1107. Driver

1108. Drizzle

1109. Drought

1110. Drum

Day-38

1111. Drummer

1112. Drumstick

1113. Drunkard

1114. Dual

1115. Dubbing

1116. Dubious

1117. Duck

1118. Due

1119. Duel

1120. Duet

1121. Duke

1122. Dumb

1123. Duo

1124. Dupe

1125. Duplicate

1126. Durable

1127. During

1128. Dusk

1129. Duster

1130. Dusty

1131. Dwarf

1132. Dye

1133. Dyer

1134. Dynamic

1135. Eager

1136. Eagle

1137. Earl

1138. Earlier

1139. Earliest

1140. Early

Day-39

1141. Earth

1142. Earthquake

1143. Easier

1144. Easiest

1145. Easy

1146. Eavesdrop

1147. Echo

1148. Eclipse

1149. Ecologist

1150. Economical

1151. Economics

1152. Economist

1153. Ecosystem

1154. Ecstatic

1155. Edible

1156. Edition

1157. Editor

1158. Education

1159. Educationist

1160. Educator

1161. Eel

1162. Effect

1163. Effective

1164. Efficacy

1165. Efficient

1166. Effort

1167. Eggetarian

1168. Egoist

1169. Egotist

1170. Elbow

Day-40

1171. Elections

1172. Electrician

1173. Elementary

1174. Eleven

1175. Ellipse

1176. Embezzle

1177. Embodied

1178. Embodiment

1179. Embody

1180. Embrace

1181. Embraced

1182. Emerald

1183. Emerge

1184. Emergency

1185. Emigrant

1186. Eminent

1187. Emission

1188. Emit

1189. Emotion

1190. Emotional

1191. Empathy

1192. Emperor

1193. Emphasis

1194. Emphasise (UK) / Emphasize (USA)

1195. Emphatic

1196. Empire

1197. Employee

1198. Employer

1199. Emu

1200. En route

Day-41

1201. Encircle

1202. Encourage

1203. Endeavour (UK) / Endeavor (USA)

1204. Endurance

1205. Enemy

1206. Engine

1207. Engineer

1208. English

1209. Engrave

1210. Enhance

1211. Enjoy

1212. Enjoyable

1213. Enlighten

1214. Enmity

1215. Enough

1216. Enquiry

1217. Enrich

1218. Ensue

1219. Ensure

1220. Enterprise

1221. Entertain

1222. Entertainer

1223. Entertainment

1224. Enthusiast

1225. Entire

1226. Entitled

1227. Entrepreneur

1228. Entrepreneurial

1229. Entrust

1230. Entry

Day-42

1231. Enumerate

1232. Enumerator

1233. Envelope

1234. Environment

1235. Envisage

1236. Epic

1237. Epidemic

1238. Epiglottis

1239. Epigraph

1240. Episode

1241. Epitaph

1242. Epitome

1243. Equator

1244. Equipment

1245. Erase

1246. Eraser

1247. Errand

1248. Errata

1249. Erratic

1250. Erratum

1251. Erroneous

1252. Erstwhile

1253. Essay

1254. Essayist

1255. Essence

1256. Essential

1257. Establish

1258. Etch

1259. Ethnicity

1260. Ethyl

Day-43

1261. Euro (currency)

1262. Europe

1263. European

1264. Evaluate

1265. Evaluation

1266. Evaluator

1267. Evaporate

1268. Evaporation

1269. Evasive

1270. Evening

1271. Event

1272. Eve-teaser

1273. Eve-teasing

1274. Evidence

1275. Evolution

1276. Exact

1277. Examine

1278. Examinee

1279. Examiner

1280. Excellent

1281. Except

1282. Exceptionally

1283. Excerpt

1284. Excitement

1285. Exclamatory

1286. Exclude

1287. Exclusion

1288. Exclusive

1289. Excursion

1290. Excuse

Day-44

1291. Executioner

1292. Executive

1293. Executor

1294. Exercise

1295. Exhaustive

1296. Exhibition

1297. Existence

1298. Expand

1299. Expansion

1300. Expect

1301. Expedient

1302. Expedite

1303. Expenditure

1304. Expenses

1305. Expensive

1306. Experience

1307. Experiment

1308. Explorer

1309. Exponent

1310. Expository

1311. Exposure

1312. External

1313. Extravagant

1314. Extravagantly

1315. Extravaganza

1316. Extreme

1317. Extremely

1318. Extremity

1319. Facilitate

1320. Facilities

Day-45

1321. Facility

1322. Factor

1323. Factory

1324. Faint

1325. Faithful

1326. Faithfully

1327. Faithfulness

1328. Fake

1329. Falcon

1330. False

1331. Fame

1332. Familiar

1333. Famine

1334. Famous

1335. Farmer

1336. Farther

1337. Farthest

1338. Father-in-law

1339. Fault

1340. Faulty

1341. Fax

1342. Feasible

1343. Feast

1344. Feat

1345. February

1346. Fed

1347. Feed

1348. Feedback

1349. Feet

1350. Feign

Day-46

1351. Felicitate

1352. Felicitation

1353. Femur

1354. Fence

1355. Ferocious

1356. Fertile

1357. Fervent

1358. Festival

1359. Festive

1360. Fever

1361. Fiancé

1362. Fiancée

1363. Fickle

1364. Fiction

1365. Fictional

1366. Field

1367. Fierce

1368. Fifteen

1369. Figure

1370. Filariasis

1371. Filthy

1372. Final

1373. Finale

1374. Finance

1375. Financial

1376. Financier

1377. Finger

1378. Finite

1379. Fire

1380. Firewall

Day-47

1381. Firm

1382. Fiscal

1383. Fish

1384. Fisheries

1385. Fishes

1386. Fissure

1387. Fitness

1388. Flag

1389. Flagrant

1390. Flamboyant

1391. Flamingo

1392. Flank

1393. Flash

1394. Flautist

1395. Flavour (UK) / Flavor (USA)

1396. Flaw

1397. Flawless

1398. Flick

1399. Flight

1400. Flood

1401. Flooded

1402. Floor

1403. Floors

1404. Florist

1405. Flour

1406. Flourish

1407. Flower

1408. Fluctuate

1409. Fluent

1410. Fluently

Day-48

1411. Flute

1412. Foe

1413. Foil

1414. Follower

1415. Foot

1416. Forehead

1417. Foreign

1418. Foreigner

1419. Forest

1420. Formative

1421. Former

1422. Formula

1423. Formulae

1424. Formulate

1425. Fortunate

1426. Fortunately

1427. Forty

1428. Fossil

1429. Fought

1430. Foul

1431. Founder

1432. Fountain

1433. Four

1434. Fourfold

1435. Fourteen

1436. Fowl

1437. Fox

1438. Frame

1439. Frantic

1440. Frantically

Day-49

1441. Fraudster

1442. Freedom

1443. Freelancer

1444. French (language)

1445. Frequently

1446. Friday

1447. Friend

1448. Frighten

1449. Frivolous

1450. Frog

1451. Frost

1452. Frown

1453. Fruit

1454. Fruitful

1455. Fruitfulness

1456. Fruitless

1457. Fuel

1458. Fulfil (UK) / Fulfill (USA)

1459. Function

1460. Functional

1461. Fundamental

1462. Fungi

1463. Fungus

1464. Furniture

1465. Further

1466. Fuse

1467. Futile

1468. Future

1469. Futuristic

1470. Gait

Day-50

1471. Gallant

1472. Gallantry

1473. Galore

1474. Gamble

1475. Gambler

1476. Gangman

1477. Gangmen

1478. Gangrene

1479. Gaol

1480. Gardener

1481. Garlic

1482. Gas

1483. Gaseous

1484. Gases

1485. Gastric

1486. Gastritis

1487. Gastroenterologist

1488. Gastroenterology

1489. Gauge

1490. Gaze

1491. Gazette

1492. Gear

1493. Gecko

1494. Geese

1495. General

1496. Generate

1497. Generation

1498. Generic

1499. Generosity

1500. Generous

Day-51

1501. Genius

1502. Genre

1503. Gentle

1504. Genuine

1505. Geography

1506. Geometry

1507. Germination

1508. Gerontology

1509. Gestation

1510. Gesture

1511. Gherkin

1512. Ghost

1513. Ghost writer

1514. Giddy

1515. Gild

1516. Gimmick

1517. Ginger

1518. Giraffe

1519. Gist

1520. Glacier

1521. Glance

1522. Glass

1523. Glean

1524. Gloss

1525. Glossary

1526. Glue

1527. Glutton

1528. Goal

1529. Goat

1530. Goldfish

Day-52

1531. Golfer

1532. Good bye

1533. Goodies

1534. Goose

1535. Gorgeous

1536. Gorilla

1537. Governance

1538. Government

1539. Governor

1540. Gracious

1541. Grade

1542. Gradual

1543. Gradually

1544. Graduate

1545. Graduation

1546. Grammar

1547. Grammarian

1548. Gramophone

1549. Granny

1550. Grape

1551. Grass

1552. Grasshopper

1553. Grate

1554. Grateful

1555. Grave

1556. Graveyard

1557. Grease

1558. Greasy

1559. Great

1560. Greed

Day-53

1561. Greedy

1562. Green

1563. Greenery

1564. Greeting

1565. Grey

1566. Grief

1567. Grieve

1568. Groom

1569. Groundnut

1570. Group

1571. Growth

1572. Grudge

1573. Guage

1574. Guarantee

1575. Guard

1576. Guava

1577. Guest

1578. Guests

1579. Guide

1580. Guild

1581. Guilt

1582. Guilty

1583. Guitar

1584. Guitarist

1585. Gum

1586. Gut

1587. Gymnasium

1588. Gymnast

1589. Gynaecologist

1590. Gynaecology

Day-54

1591. Habit

1592. Habitual

1593. Hacker

1594. Haemoglobin

1595. Haemorrhage (UK) / Hemorrhage

(USA)

1596. Hailstorm

1597. Half

1598. Halves

1599. Hammer

1600. Hamster

1601. Handicapped

1602. Handkerchief

1603. Handle

1604. Handloom

1605. Handsome

1606. Handy

1607. Hanger

1608. Haptics

1609. Harass

1610. Harassment

1611. Harbour (UK) / Harbor (USA)

1612. Hardware

1613. Hare

1614. Harmonica (mouth organ)

1615. Harmonicist

1616. Harvest

1617. Hatred

1618. Haughty

1619. Hawk

1620. Hazard

Day-55

1621. Hazardous

1622. Headed

1623. Headman

1624. Heal

1625. Health

1626. Healthy

1627. Hear

1628. Heard

1629. Heart

1630. Heartthrob

1631. Heaven

1632. Heavily

1633. Heavy

1634. Hedgehog

1635. Heel

1636. Height

1637. Hell

1638. Hello

1639. Hence

1640. Herbivore

1641. Herbivorous

1642. Herd

1643. Hereditary

1644. Herewith

1645. Herring

1646. Highlight

1647. Hiker

1648. Hindi (language)

1649. Hippopotamus

1650. History

Day-56

1651. Hoard

1652. Hockey

1653. Hoist

1654. Hole

1655. Hollow

1656. Holy

1657. Homeopath

1658. Homeopathy

1659. Homograph

1660. Homonym

1661. Homophone

1662. Hone

1663. Honesty

1664. Honey

1665. Honorarium

1666. Honorary

1667. Hook

1668. Horde

1669. Hornbill

1670. Horrible

1671. Horrific

1672. Hospitable

1673. Hospital

1674. Hospitality

1675. Host

1676. Hostess

1677. However

1678. Hug

1679. Hugged

1680. Human

Day-57

1681. Humane

1682. Humanities

1683. Humanity

1684. Humble

1685. Humid

1686. Humidity

1687. Humiliate

1688. Humiliation

1689. Humility

1690. Humming bird

1691. Hundred

1692. Hunger

1693. Hungry

1694. Hurried

1695. Hurriedly

1696. Hurry

1697. Hush

1698. Hydroelectric

1699. Hymn

1700. Hypocrisy

1701. Hypocrite

1702. Iceberg

1703. Idiot

1704. Idiotic

1705. Idle

1706. Idly

1707. Idol

1708. Ignorance

1709. Ignorant

1710. Illegal

Day-58

1711. Illegitimate

1712. Illicit

1713. Illness

1714. Illogical

1715. Illusion

1716. Imaginary

1717. Imagination

1718. Imagine

1719. Imitate

1720. Immense

1721. Immensely

1722. Immigrant

1723. Immigration

1724. Immune

1725. Immunity

1726. Immunology

1727. Impact

1728. Impair

1729. Impartial

1730. Imperative

1731. Imperial

1732. Imperious

1733. Impersonate

1734. Impose

1735. Impossible

1736. Impression

1737. Impressive

1738. Improve

1739. Inactive

1740. Inaugurate

Day-59

1741. Inauguration

1742. Incident

1743. Include

1744. Inclusion

1745. Inclusive

1746. Income

1747. Independence

1748. Independent

1749. Independently

1750. Index

1751. Indigenous

1752. Indolent

1753. Induction

1754. Industrial

1755. Industrialist

1756. Industrious

1757. Industry

1758. Infancy

1759. Infant

1760. Inferior

1761. Infinite

1762. Infirm

1763. Infirmary

1764. Inform

1765. Information

1766. Informative

1767. Informer

1768. Infrastructure

1769. Ingredients

1770. Inhabitant

Day-60

1771. Inheritance

1772. Initiative

1773. Injection

1774. Injuries

1775. Injury

1776. In-laws

1777. Inn

1778. Innate

1779. Innings

1780. Innocence

1781. Innocent

1782. Innumerable

1783. Inordinate

1784. Inquiries

1785. Inquiry

1786. Inquisitive

1787. Insolvency

1788. Insolvent

1789. Install

1790. Instalment (UK) / Installment (USA)

1791. Instance

1792. Instant

1793. Instead

1794. Instinct

1795. Instrumental

1796. Integrate

1797. Integration

1798. Integrity

1799. Intellect

1800. Intellectual

Day-61

1801. Intelligible

1802. Intense

1803. Intensity

1804. Intensive

1805. Inter college

1806. Interact

1807. Interaction

1808. Interactive

1809. Interfere

1810. Interjection

1811. Intermediary

1812. Intermediate

1813. Intermittent

1814. Intermittently

1815. Internal

1816. Internally

1817. International

1818. Internet

1819. Interpret

1820. Interpretation

1821. Interrogate

1822. Interrogation

1823. Interrogative

1824. Interrupt

1825. Interruption

1826. Intervene

1827. Interview

1828. Interviewee

1829. Interviewer

1830. Intestine

Day-62

1831. Intimacy

1832. Intimate

1833. Intonation

1834. Intra college

1835. Intrepid

1836. Intricate

1837. Introduction

1838. Introductory

1839. Intrude

1840. Intruder

1841. Invade

1842. Invader

1843. Invasion

1844. Invent

1845. Invention

1846. Inventor

1847. Invest

1848. Investigate

1849. Investigation

1850. Investigator

1851. Investment

1852. Investor

1853. Ion

1854. Ionosphere

1855. Iris

1856. Iron

1857. Ironic

1858. Irony

1859. Irresponsible

1860. Island

Day-63

1861. Issue

1862. Item

1863. Itinerary

1864. Jackal

1865. Jacket

1866. Jade

1867. Jaggery

1868. Jaguar

1869. Jailer

1870. January (month)

1871. Jargon

1872. Jaw

1873. Jealous

1874. Jealousy

1875. Jeep

1876. Jester

1877. Jockey

1878. Jog

1879. Jogging

1880. Joule

1881. Journal

1882. Journalist

1883. Journey

1884. Jubilant

1885. Jubilee

1886. Judge

1887. Judgement

1888. Judiciary

1889. Judicious

1890. July (month)

Day-64

1891. Jump

1892. June (month)

1893. Jungle

1894. Junior

1895. Junk

1896. Jupiter (planet)

1897. Justice

1898. Kangaroo

1899. Keen

1900. Kennel

1901. Keyboard

1902. Kick

1903. Kicked

1904. Kid

1905. Kidney

1906. Kin

1907. Kinder

1908. Kindergarten

1909. Kindle

1910. Kindred

1911. Kinesics

1912. Kinetic

1913. Kitchen

1914. Kite

1915. Kith

1916. Knave

1917. Knee

1918. Kneel

1919. Knelt

1920. Knight

Day-65

1921. Knit

1922. Knives

1923. Knock

1924. Know

1925. Knowledge

1926. Knowledgeable

1927. Knowledgeably

1928. Labour (UK) / Labor (USA)

1929. Labourer (UK) / Laborer (USA)

1930. Lactarian

1931. Lactic

1932. Lactose

1933. Ladder

1934. Ladle

1935. Laid

1936. Lain

1937. Lake

1938. Lakh

1939. Landlady

1940. Landlord

1941. Landmark

1942. Landscape

1943. Landslide

1944. Lane

1945. Language

1946. Larva (singular)

1947. Larvae (plural)

1948. Larynx

1949. Later (= in the future)

1950. Latitude

Day-66

1951. Latter (= the second one)

1952. Lattice

1953. Laud

1954. Laudable

1955. Laudatory

1956. Laugh

1957. Laughable

1958. Launch

1959. Laurel

1960. Lavender

1961. Lawless

1962. Lawn

1963. Lawyer

1964. Lay

1965. Layman

1966. Laymen

1967. Laziness

1968. Lazy

1969. Lead

1970. Leader

1971. Leaf

1972. Leaflet

1973. Leafy

1974. Leak

1975. Leaves

1976. Led

1977. Leech

1978. Leek (vegetable)

1979. Legacy

1980. Legal

Day-67

1981. Legality

1982. Legally

1983. Legible

1984. Legibly

1985. Legitimate

1986. Leisure

1987. Lemonade

1988. Lend

1989. Lender

1990. Length

1991. Lenient

1992. Lent

1993. Leopard

1994. Lessen

1995. Lesson

1996. Level

1997. Levelled

1998. Lever

1999. Leverage

2000. Levied

2001. Levies

2002. Levy

2003. Liabilities

2004. Liability

2005. Lice

2006. Lie

2007. Lieutenant

2008. Light

2009. Linguist

2010. Linguistics

Day-68

2011. Lion (male)

2012. Lioness (female)

2013. Liquid

2014. Lit

2015. Lite (denoting low-fat or low-sugar)

2016. Litre (UK) / Liter (USA)

2017. Litter (= rubbish such as cans, bottles, paper, etc.)

2018. Liver

2019. Lizard

2020. Loaf

2021. Loafer

2022. Loan

2023. Lobe

2024. Lock

2025. Locker

2026. Locket

2027. Locomotive

2028. Loco-pilot

2029. Lodge

2030. Lofty

2031. Logical

2032. Logistics

2033. Londoner

2034. Lonely

2035. Longitude

2036. Look alike

2037. Loose

2038. Lose

2039. Loss

2040. Loudspeaker

Day-69

2041. Lousy

2042. Lovable

2043. Love

2044. Lover

2045. Lovingly

2046. Loyal

2047. Lucrative

2048. Luggage

2049. Lukewarm

2050. Lump

2051. Lunacy

2052. Lunar

2053. Lunatic

2054. Lunch

2055. Lush

2056. Luxuriant

2057. Luxuriantly

2058. Luxurious

2059. Luxury

2060. Lynx

2061. Lyric

2062. Lyricist

2063. Lyrics

2064. Macaw

2065. Mace

2066. Machine

2067. Machinery

2068. Magazine

2069. Magic

2070. Magical

Day-70

2071. Magician

2072. Magna Carta

2073. Magnanimity

2074. Magnanimous

2075. Magnesium

2076. Magnet

2077. Magnetic

2078. Magnitude

2079. Magnum opus

2080. Maid (= a female servant)

2081. Maiden (= an unmarried girl / young woman)

2082. Mailman

2083. Main

2084. Maintain

2085. Maintenance

2086. Maize

2087. Majestic

2088. Major

2089. Majority

2090. Malaprop

2091. Malapropism

2092. Malaria

2093. Malevolent

2094. Malign

2095. Malignant

2096. Mammal

2097. Mammoth

2098. Manageable

2099. Mandarin (language)

2100. Mandatory

Day-71

2101. Mane (= hair on the neck of a horse)

2102. Manganese

2103. Mangled

2104. Mango

2105. Mangoes

2106. Manifest

2107. Mannequin

2108. Manners

2109. Manoeuvre

2110. Mansion

2111. Mantel (= a shelf above a fireplace)

2112. Mantle (= a part of the earth below the surface)

2113. Manual

2114. Manually

2115. Manufacture

2116. Manufacturer

2117. Manure

2118. Mar

2119. Marble

2120. March (month)

2121. Mare

2122. Marker

2123. Maroon

2124. Marred

2125. Marriage

2126. Married

2127. Marrow

2128. Marry

2129. Mars (planet)

2130. Marshal

Day-72

2131. Marvel

2132. Marvellous (UK) / Marvelous (USA)

2133. Mason

2134. Mass

2135. Massacre

2136. Massive

2137. Mastermind

2138. Masterpiece

2139. Maternal

2140. Matrices

2141. Matrimonial

2142. Matrimony

2143. Matrix

2144. Mausoleum

2145. May (month)

2146. Maze

2147. Meagre

2148. Mean

2149. Meant

2150. Meanwhile

2151. Measure

2152. Meat

2153. Mechanic

2154. Media

2155. Mediate

2156. Mediator

2157. Mediocre

2158. Meditate

2159. Meditation

2160. Medium

Day-73

2161. Meek

2162. Meekness

2163. Meet

2164. Member

2165. Membership

2166. Membrane

2167. Memento

2168. Memo

2169. Memoir

2170. Memoirist

2171. Memoranda

2172. Memorandum

2173. Memory

2174. Mensuration

2175. Mention

2176. Mercury (planet)

2177. Mere

2178. Merely

2179. Merit

2180. Meritorious

2181. Meritoriously

2182. Mesosphere

2183. Message

2184. Met

2185. Metabolism

2186. Metaphor

2187. Methodology

2188. Mic

2189. Mice

2190. Microphone (= mic)

Day-74

2191. Microscope

2192. Microwave

2193. Middle

2194. Migraine

2195. Migrant

2196. Migration

2197. Milker

2198. Milkman

2199. Mill

2200. Miller

2201. Million

2202. Millionaire

2203. Millipede

2204. Mimic

2205. Mimicry

2206. Miner (= a labourer who works in a
mine)

2207. Mingle

2208. Mining

2209. Minister

2210. Ministry

2211. Minor

2212. Mint

2213. Minute

2214. Miracle

2215. Mirage

2216. Mire

2217. Misappropriate

2218. Miscellaneous

2219. Mischief

2220. Mischievous

Day-75

2221. Miser

2222. Misery

2223. Missionaries

2224. Missionary

2225. Mistake

2226. Mister

2227. Mistress

2228. Mnemonic

2229. Moat

2230. Mock

2231. Mocker

2232. Modal auxiliaries

2233. Model

2234. Modem

2235. Moderator

2236. Modern

2237. Modest

2238. Modulation

2239. Module

2240. Moist

2241. Mole

2242. Molecule

2243. Moment

2244. Momentous

2245. Monarch

2246. Monarchy

2247. Monday

2248. Money

2249. Monk

2250. Monkey

Day-76

2251. Monopoly

2252. Monotonous

2253. Monotony

2254. Monsoon

2255. Monster

2256. Monument

2257. Moon

2258. Moose

2259. Mop

2260. Mopped

2261. Moral

2262. Morale

2263. Morning

2264. Morpheme

2265. Mortgage

2266. Mosquito

2267. Mosquitoes

2268. Mother-in-law

2269. Mothers-in-law

2270. Motif

2271. Motifs

2272. Motivate

2273. Motivator

2274. Motive

2275. Motives

2276. Mourn

2277. Mourning (= the expression of sorrow

for the death of a person)

2278. Mouse

2279. Mouth Organ

2280. Mouth Organist

Day-77

2281. Movement

2282. Mover

2283. Mucus

2284. Mulberry

2285. Mule

2286. Multiple

2287. Multiplication

2288. Multiply

2289. Murmur

2290. Muscle

2291. Muscular

2292. Muse

2293. Museum

2294. Musician

2295. Muslin

2296. Mutter

2297. Muzzle

2298. Myna

2299. Myriad

2300. Mysterious

2301. Mystery

2302. Nail

2303. Naïve

2304. Nanny

2305. Narcissistic

2306. Narrow

2307. Nasal

2308. Nasty

2309. Nation

2310. National

Day-78

2311. Nationalist

2312. Nationality

2313. Native

2314. Natural

2315. Nature

2316. Naughty

2317. Nausea

2318. Navel

2319. Navy

2320. Necessary

2321. Necessity

2322. Needful

2323. Needy

2324. Neem

2325. Negative

2326. Neighbour (UK) / Neighbor (USA)

2327. Neighbourhood (UK) / Neighborhood
(USA)

2328. Nephew

2329. Nephrologist

2330. Nephrology

2331. Neptune (planet)

2332. Nerve

2333. Nerves

2334. Nervous

2335. Nevertheless

2336. Newbie

2337. Niece

2338. Night

2339. Nightingale

2340. Nightmare

Day-79

2341. Nil

2342. Nine

2343. Nineteen

2344. Ninety

2345. Nitrogen

2346. Noble

2347. Nocturnal

2348. Nod

2349. Nodded

2350. Noise

2351. Noisy

2352. Nomad

2353. Nomadic

2354. Nomenclature

2355. Nominal

2356. Nominate

2357. Nomination

2358. Nominee

2359. Nonetheless

2360. Nonuple

2361. Non-vegetarian

2362. Norm

2363. Normal

2364. Nostril

2365. Notice

2366. Notification

2367. Notify

2368. Notion

2369. Notorious

2370. Noun

Day-80

2371. Novel

2372. Novelty

2373. November (month)

2374. Novice

2375. Nullify

2376. Numerous

2377. Numismatics

2378. Nutrition

2379. Oar

2380. Oasis

2381. Oath

2382. Obedient

2383. Obediently

2384. Obese

2385. Obesity

2386. Obey

2387. Object

2388. Objectionable

2389. Objective

2390. Obligation

2391. Oblige

2392. Obliterate

2393. Obnoxious

2394. Obvious

2395. Obviously

2396. Occasion

2397. Occupation

2398. Occur

2399. Occurrence

2400. Ocean

Day-81

2401. Octagon

2402. Octagonal

2403. October (month)

2404. Octogenarian

2405. Octopus

2406. Octuple

2407. Odd

2408. Oddly

2409. Ode

2410. Odour (UK) / Odor (USA)

2411. Offend

2412. Offense (UK) / Offence (USA)

2413. Offensive

2414. Offspring

2415. Often

2416. Ointment

2417. Olympic

2418. Ombudsman

2419. Omelette (UK) / Omelet (USA)

2420. Omnivore

2421. Omnivorous

2422. Onion

2423. Onslaught

2424. Oops

2425. Opaque

2426. Operation

2427. Opponent

2428. Opportune

2429. Opportunistic

2430. Opportunities

Day-82

2431. Opportunity

2432. Oppress

2433. Oppressive

2434. Oppressor

2435. Optative

2436. Optics

2437. Optimism

2438. Optimist

2439. Optimistic

2440. Optimum

2441. Option

2442. Optional

2443. Orangutan

2444. Orator

2445. Oratory

2446. Order

2447. Ore

2448. Organ

2449. Organic

2450. Organisation (UK) / Organization
(USA)

2451. Organisational (UK) / Organizational
(USA)

2452. Organise (UK) / Organize (USA)

2453. Origin

2454. Original

2455. Orthopaedic (UK) / Orthopedic (USA)

2456. Ostrich

2457. Ought

2458. Outflow

2459. Oven

2460. Overload

Day-83

2461. Overwhelm

2462. Overwhelming

2463. Owe

2464. Owl

2465. Own

2466. Owner

2467. Ox

2468. Oxen

2469. Oxygen

2470. Oxymoron

2471. Oyster

2472. Pace

2473. Pacific

2474. Pacifier

2475. Pacify

2476. Packet

2477. Paddy

2478. Paediatrician (UK) / Pediatrician (USA)

2479. Painter

2480. Paisa

2481. Palindrome

2482. Palm

2483. Palmist

2484. Palmistry

2485. Pamphlet

2486. Pamphleteer

2487. Pan

2488. Pancreas

2489. Panda

2490. Pandemic

Day84

2491. Pandemonium

2492. Pang

2493. Panorama

2494. Panther

2495. Par

2496. Paralanguage

2497. Parallel

2498. Parameter

2499. Paranoia

2500. Paranoid

2501. Parasite

2502. Pardon

2503. Pardoner

2504. Parliament

2505. Parliamentarian

2506. Parliamentary

2507. Parrot

2508. Partial

2509. Partiality

2510. Partially

2511. Participant

2512. Participation

2513. Particular

2514. Partner

2515. Partnership

2516. Passerby

2517. Passersby

2518. Passion

2519. Passionate

2520. Pasta

Day-85

2521. Paste

2522. Pastor

2523. Pat

2524. Patch

2525. Paternal

2526. Pathologist

2527. Pathology

2528. Patriot

2529. Patriotic

2530. Patriotism

2531. Patrol

2532. Patrolled

2533. Patted

2534. Pause

2535. Pavilion

2536. Pay

2537. Payee

2538. Payer

2539. Payment

2540. Peace

2541. Peaceful

2542. Peacock

2543. Peahen

2544. Pear

2545. Pearl

2546. Peasant

2547. Pedal

2548. Pedlar

2549. Peer

2550. Pelican

Day-86

2551. Pencil

2552. Penguin

2553. Penicillin

2554. Peninsula

2555. Penniless

2556. Penny

2557. Pension

2558. Pensioner

2559. People

2560. Pepper

2561. Per cent

2562. Perceive

2563. Percentage

2564. Percentile

2565. Perception

2566. Perennial

2567. Perfect

2568. Perfection

2569. Perfume

2570. Perhaps

2571. Perihelion

2572. Period

2573. Peripheral

2574. Perk

2575. Perpendicular

2576. Perpetual

2577. Person

2578. Personification

2579. Perspiration

2580. Persuade

Day-87

2581. Persuasion

2582. Persuasive

2583. Perusal

2584. Pervasive

2585. Pessimism

2586. Pessimist

2587. Pessimistic

2588. Petition

2589. Petitioner

2590. Petrol

2591. Petroleum

2592. Pharynx

2593. Philanthropist

2594. Philanthropy

2595. Philosopher

2596. Philosophy

2597. Phobia

2598. Phobic

2599. Phosphate

2600. Phosphorus

2601. Photo

2602. Photogenic

2603. Photograph

2604. Photos

2605. Photosynthesis

2606. Phrase

2607. Physician

2608. Physicist

2609. Physiology

2610. Physiotherapist

Day-88

2611. Physiotherapy

2612. Physique

2613. Pianist

2614. Piano

2615. Pic

2616. Pick

2617. Pickle

2618. Pickpocket

2619. Picture

2620. Picturesque

2621. Pie

2622. Piety

2623. Pigeon

2624. Pike

2625. Pilgrim

2626. Pilgrimage

2627. Pilot

2628. Pineapple

2629. Pioneer

2630. Pious

2631. Pipette

2632. Pitch

2633. Pivot

2634. Pivotal

2635. Plain

2636. Plaintiff

2637. Plait

2638. Plane

2639. Planning

2640. Plaster

Day-89

2641. Plastic

2642. Platform

2643. Platinum

2644. Plausible

2645. Pleader

2646. Pleasure

2647. Pledge

2648. Pluck

2649. Plumber

2650. Plural

2651. Pluto

2652. Plywood

2653. Pocket

2654. Poem

2655. Poet

2656. Poetess (= a female poet)

2657. Poignant

2658. Poison

2659. Poisonous

2660. Poke

2661. Police

2662. Policeman

2663. Policemen

2664. Policies

2665. Policy

2666. Polished

2667. Polite

2668. Politician

2669. Politics

2670. Polity

Day-90

2671. Polyandry

2672. Polybags

2673. Polygamy

2674. Polyglot

2675. Polygon

2676. Pond

2677. Pope

2678. Popular

2679. Population

2680. Porcupine

2681. Pore

2682. Pores

2683. Porous

2684. Positive

2685. Possessive

2686. Possible

2687. Postal

2688. Postman

2689. Postpone

2690. Potassium

2691. Potato

2692. Potatoes

2693. Potent

2694. Potential

2695. Poultry

2696. Pound (currency)

2697. Pour

2698. Poverty

2699. Practice

2700. Practise (verb) (UK) / Practice (USA)

Day-91

2701. Practitioner

2702. Praise

2703. Pray

2704. Preach

2705. Preacher

2706. Precarious

2707. Precaution

2708. Precede

2709. Precept

2710. Precious

2711. Precipitate

2712. Precise

2713. Predator

2714. Predecessor

2715. Predict

2716. Predictable

2717. Prefer

2718. Prefix

2719. Pregnancy

2720. Pregnant

2721. Prejudiced

2722. Premature

2723. Premises

2724. Preoccupied

2725. Preposition

2726. Prequel

2727. Pre-requisites

2728. Presentation

2729. Presenter

2730. Preservative

Day-92

2731. Preserve

2732. Preside

2733. Presidency

2734. President

2735. Presidential

2736. Pressure

2737. Presume

2738. Presumption

2739. Pretext

2740. Pretty

2741. Prevalent

2742. Prevention

2743. Previous

2744. Previously

2745. Prey

2746. Price

2747. Pride

2748. Priest

2749. Priestess (= a female priest)

2750. Prince

2751. Princes

2752. Princess

2753. Princesses

2754. Principal

2755. Principle

2756. Print

2757. Prize

2758. Proactive

2759. Probability

2760. Procedure

Day-93

2761. Proceed

2762. Process

2763. Procession

2764. Processor

2765. Procrastinate

2766. Procrastination

2767. Proctor

2768. Prodigy

2769. Produce

2770. Producer

2771. Product

2772. Production

2773. Profession

2774. Professor

2775. Progenitor

2776. Programme (UK) / Program (USA)

2777. Progress

2778. Progression

2779. Progressive

2780. Prohibit

2781. Prohibition

2782. Project

2783. Prolific

2784. Prominent

2785. Promising

2786. Promissory

2787. Prone

2788. Pronoun

2789. Pronounce

2790. Pronunciation

Day-94

2791. Proof

2792. Proofreader

2793. Properly

2794. Prophet

2795. Proponent

2796. Proposal

2797. Propriety

2798. Pros

2799. Prospect

2800. Prospectus

2801. Prosper

2802. Prosperity

2803. Prosperous

2804. Protein

2805. Protest

2806. Protestant

2807. Protocol

2808. Prototype

2809. Protractor

2810. Proud

2811. Proverb

2812. Providence

2813. Provident

2814. Provider

2815. Province

2816. Provision

2817. Proxemics

2818. Proximity

2819. Proxy

2820. Psalm

Day-95

2821. Psephologist

2822. Psephology

2823. Pseudonym

2824. Psychiatrist

2825. Psychiatry

2826. Psychic

2827. Psycho

2828. Psychologist

2829. Psychology

2830. Psychopath

2831. Psychotherapist

2832. Psychotherapy

2833. Publisher

2834. Puff

2835. Pulmonologist

2836. Pulmonology

2837. Pulse

2838. Puma

2839. Pungent

2840. Punishment

2841. Pupil

2842. Puppet

2843. Purchase

2844. Purchaser

2845. Pure

2846. Purity

2847. Purpose

2848. Purview

2849. Pyramid

2850. Quadruple

Day-96

2851. Quail

2852. Qualification

2853. Qualify

2854. Quality

2855. Quantity

2856. Quantum

2857. Quarrel

2858. Quarrelsome

2859. Queen

2860. Query

2861. Question

2862. Questionnaire

2863. Queue

2864. Quiet

2865. Quietly

2866. Quintessence

2867. Quintuple

2868. Quintuplet

2869. Quit

2870. Quite

2871. Rabbit

2872. Rack

2873. Racket

2874. Radical

2875. Radii

2876. Radio

2877. Radius

2878. Rag

2879. Rage

2880. Ragged

Day-97

2881. Ragger

2882. Ragging

2883. Raid

2884. Rail

2885. Railway

2886. Rampant

2887. Range

2888. Ranger

2889. Rapper

2890. Rapport

2891. Rare

2892. Rarely

2893. Rascal

2894. Rat

2895. Ratio

2896. Ration

2897. Rational

2898. Rationale

2899. Rationalist

2900. Reader

2901. Realm

2902. Reap

2903. Rear

2904. Reason

2905. Reasonable

2906. Rebel

2907. Rebelled

2908. Rebellion

2909. Receipt

2910. Receive

Day-98

2911. Receiver

2912. Recent

2913. Recently

2914. Reception

2915. Receptionist

2916. Recipe

2917. Recipient

2918. Recognise (UK) / Recognize (USA)

2919. Recognition

2920. Recommend

2921. Recommendation

2922. Recreate

2923. Rector

2924. Recyclable

2925. Recycle

2926. Reduce

2927. Redundant

2928. Reef

2929. Referee

2930. Reference

2931. Reflect

2932. Reflection

2933. Reflex

2934. Reflexive

2935. Refract

2936. Refraction

2937. Refrain

2938. Refrigerant

2939. Refrigerate

2940. Refrigerator

Day-99

2941. Refuge

2942. Refugee

2943. Regal

2944. Regards

2945. Register

2946. Registrar

2947. Registration

2948. Registry

2949. Relation

2950. Relationship

2951. Relative

2952. Relax

2953. Relaxation

2954. Relay

2955. Relevance

2956. Relevant

2957. Reliable

2958. Relic

2959. Relief

2960. Relies

2961. Relieve

2962. Relieved

2963. Reliever

2964. Religion

2965. Rely

2966. Remain

2967. Remainder

2968. Remedial

2969. Remedy

2970. Remind

Day-100

2971. Reminder

2972. Reminiscence

2973. Reminiscent

2974. Remission

2975. Remit

2976. Remitted

2977. Remnant

2978. Remnants

2979. Remorse

2980. Remote

2981. Remuneration

2982. Renew

2983. Renewable

2984. Renewal

2985. Rent

2986. Rental

2987. Repair

2988. Repeat

2989. Repetition

2990. Replacement

2991. Replies

2992. Reply

2993. Report

2994. Reporter

2995. Representation

2996. Representative

2997. Reptile

2998. Republic

2999. Reputation

3000. Reputed

Day-101

3001. Request

3002. Rescue

3003. Rescuer

3004. Research

3005. Resemblance

3006. Resemble

3007. Reservation

3008. Reserved

3009. Residence

3010. Residency

3011. Resident

3012. Residential

3013. Residual

3014. Residue

3015. Resist

3016. Resistance

3017. Resonate

3018. Resources

3019. Respect

3020. Respectable

3021. Respectful

3022. Respectfully

3023. Respective

3024. Respectively

3025. Respond

3026. Respondent

3027. Response

3028. Responsibility

3029. Responsible

3030. Responsive

Day-102

3031. Rest

3032. Restaurant

3033. Restaurateur

3034. Resume

3035. Retail

3036. Retailer

3037. Retain

3038. Retaliate

3039. Retaliation

3040. Retaliator

3041. Retire

3042. Retiree

3043. Retirement

3044. Retreat

3045. Return

3046. Reusable

3047. Reveal

3048. Revenge

3049. Revenue

3050. Revere

3051. Revered

3052. Revert

3053. Review

3054. Reviewer

3055. Reward

3056. Rhetoric

3057. Rhombus

3058. Rhyme

3059. Rhythm

3060. Rhythmic

Day-103

3061. Rhythmically

3062. Ribbon

3063. Rice

3064. Riches

3065. Richness

3066. Ride

3067. Rider

3068. Rigger

3069. Rigging

3070. Ripe

3071. Ripen

3072. Ripened

3073. Risk

3074. Rival

3075. Rivalry

3076. Rivals

3077. Road

3078. Roast

3079. Roasted

3080. Robber

3081. Robbery

3082. Robin

3083. Robot

3084. Robotics

3085. Robust

3086. Rocky

3087. Rocket

3088. Rode

3089. Rodent

3090. Rogue

Day-104

3091. Role Model

3092. Roommate

3093. Rooster

3094. Root

3095. Rouge

3096. Rough

3097. Route

3098. Routine

3099. Row

3100. Royal

3101. Royalty

3102. Rubber

3103. Rubel (currency)

3104. Ruby

3105. Rug

3106. Rugby

3107. Rugged

3108. Rule

3109. Ruled

3110. Ruler

3111. Ruling

3112. Run

3113. Runner

3114. Running

3115. Runway

3116. Rupee (currency)

3117. Rupture

3118. Rural

3119. Rustic

3120. Sachet

Day-105

3121. Sack

3122. Sacred

3123. Sacrifice

3124. Salamander

3125. Salaried

3126. Salaries

3127. Salary

3128. Salesman

3129. Salmon (fish)

3130. Salty

3131. Salvation

3132. Same

3133. Sanction

3134. Sanctuary

3135. Sandal

3136. Sane

3137. Sang

3138. Sanity

3139. Sarcasm

3140. Sarcastic

3141. Sardine

3142. Sat

3143. Sate

3144. Satellite

3145. Satiate

3146. Satiated

3147. Satire

3148. Satisfaction

3149. Satisfactory

3150. Satisfy

Day-106

3151. Satisfying

3152. Saturated

3153. Saturation

3154. Saturday

3155. Saturn (planet)

3156. Sauce

3157. Saviour (UK) / Savior (USA)

3158. Saxophone

3159. Scale

3160. Scam

3161. Scammer

3162. Scanty

3163. Scarce

3164. Scarcity

3165. Scare

3166. Scarlet

3167. Scavenger

3168. Scenario

3169. Scene

3170. Scenery

3171. Scent

3172. Sceptical (UK) / Skeptical (USA)

3173. Scheme

3174. Schemer

3175. Schizophrenia

3176. School

3177. Scholar

3178. Scholarship

3179. Sciatica

3180. Scientist

Day-107

3181. Scintillate

3182. Scissors

3183. Score

3184. Scorn

3185. Scornful

3186. Scorpion

3187. Scorpions

3188. Scoundrel

3189. Scout

3190. Scratch

3191. Screen

3192. Scrutinise (UK) / Scrutinize (USA)

3193. Scrutiny

3194. Sculpt

3195. Sculptor

3196. Sculpture

3197. Seal

3198. Sealing

3199. Season

3200. Seasoned

3201. Seat

3202. Seated

3203. Second

3204. Secondary

3205. Secret

3206. Secretariat

3207. Secretary

3208. Secretly

3209. Sect

3210. Sectarian

Day-108

3211. Section

3212. Sector

3213. Sedentary

3214. Seed

3215. Seek

3216. Seer

3217. Segment

3218. Seismic

3219. Seizure

3220. Seldom

3221. Seller

3222. Semantic

3223. Seminal

3224. Seminar

3225. Senator

3226. Sender

3227. Senior

3228. Sensational

3229. Sensible

3230. Sensitive

3231. Sentry

3232. Separate

3233. Separately

3234. Separatist

3235. September (month)

3236. Septuple

3237. Sequel

3238. Sequence

3239. Sequential

3240. Serene

Day-109

3241. Sergeant

3242. Series

3243. Serious

3244. Servant

3245. Serve

3246. Server

3247. Service

3248. Sesame

3249. Seven

3250. Sever

3251. Severe

3252. Severity

3253. Sew

3254. Sextuple

3255. Shampoo

3256. Shareholder

3257. Shark

3258. Sheath

3259. Shed

3260. Sheep

3261. Shelf

3262. Shelves

3263. Shield

3264. Shift

3265. Shin

3266. Shine

3267. Shirt

3268. Shopkeeper

3269. Short

3270. Shoulder

Day-110

3271. Shun

3272. Shunned

3273. Shut

3274. Shuttle

3275. Sibling

3276. Siblings

3277. Sick

3278. Sickle

3279. Sigh

3280. Sight

3281. Sign

3282. Signal

3283. Signatory

3284. Signature

3285. Silence

3286. Silent

3287. Silhouette

3288. Simile

3289. Simple

3290. Sincere

3291. Sincerely

3292. Sincerity

3293. Sing

3294. Single

3295. Singular

3296. Sister-in-law

3297. Sit

3298. Site

3299. Sitting

3300. Situation

Day-111

3301. Sketch

3302. Sketchy

3303. Skull

3304. Slain

3305. Slam

3306. Slammed

3307. Slap

3308. Slapped

3309. Slaughter

3310. Slay

3311. Sleep

3312. Slew

3313. Slice

3314. Slices

3315. Sloth

3316. Slum

3317. Smash

3318. Smile

3319. Snake

3320. Sneak

3321. Sneeze

3322. Sniff

3323. Sniffed

3324. Snooker

3325. Snore

3326. Soap

3327. Soar

3328. Sober

3329. Socialism

3330. Socialist

Day-112

3331. Society

3332. Socket

3333. Soda

3334. Software

3335. Soil

3336. Solace

3337. Solar

3338. Sole

3339. Solemn

3340. Solemnly

3341. Solid

3342. Solidarity

3343. Solitude

3344. Solo

3345. Soluble

3346. Solution

3347. Somersault

3348. Somnambulism

3349. Somnambulist

3350. Sonnet

3351. Sonneteer

3352. Soothe

3353. Sophisticated

3354. Sore

3355. Sorrow

3356. Sorry

3357. Sought

3358. Soul

3359. Soup

3360. Sovereign

Day-113

3361. Sovereignty

3362. Sow

3363. Space

3364. Spacious

3365. Spade

3366. Spam

3367. Spare

3368. Sparrow

3369. Spear

3370. Special

3371. Specialised (UK) / Specialized (USA)

3372. Speciality (UK) / Specialty (USA)

3373. Species

3374. Specs

3375. Spectacles

3376. Spectacular

3377. Spectator

3378. Spectators

3379. Spectra

3380. Spectrum

3381. Speculate

3382. Speculation

3383. Spend

3384. Spendthrift

3385. Spent

3386. Sphygmomanometer

3387. Spider

3388. Spin

3389. Spine

3390. Spinner

Day-114

3391. Spirit

3392. Spiritual

3393. Spirometer

3394. Spite

3395. Spiteful

3396. Spoof

3397. Spoon

3398. Spouse

3399. Spray

3400. Spread

3401. Sprinter

3402. Squabble

3403. Squad

3404. Square

3405. Squirrel

3406. Stag

3407. Stage

3408. Stagnant

3409. Stair

3410. Staircase

3411. Stakeholder

3412. Stale

3413. Stalk

3414. Stall

3415. Stamina

3416. Stammer

3417. Stamp

3418. Stampede

3419. Stance

3420. Standard

Day-115

3421. Standardisation (UK) / Standardization (USA)

3422. Stanza

3423. Starch

3424. Stardom

3425. Stare

3426. Stark

3427. Starling

3428. Starrer

3429. Starry

3430. Startled

3431. Starvation

3432. Starve

3433. Static

3434. Station

3435. Stationary

3436. Stationery

3437. Statistics

3438. Stature

3439. Status

3440. Status quo

3441. Stealth

3442. Steep

3443. Stem

3444. Stent

3445. Stereotype

3446. Sterilise (UK) / Sterilize (USA)

3447. Stethoscope

3448. Stigma

3449. Stile

3450. Stimulate

Day-116

3451. Stimulus

3452. Stipend

3453. Stir

3454. Stirred

3455. Stitch

3456. Stock

3457. Stockist

3458. Stoic

3459. Stoicism

3460. Stomach

3461. Stomata

3462. Storey (= floor)

3463. Storeyed

3464. Storeys (= floors)

3465. Stories

3466. Storm

3467. Story

3468. Stout

3469. Straight

3470. Strain

3471. Strand

3472. Strange

3473. Strangely

3474. Strategic

3475. Strategist

3476. Strategy

3477. Stratosphere

3478. Streak

3479. Stream

3480. Street

Day-117

3481. Stress

3482. Stubborn

3483. Stuck

3484. Stump

3485. Stun

3486. Stunned

3487. Stunning

3488. Stunt

3489. Stuntman

3490. Sturdy

3491. Stutter

3492. Style

3493. Subject

3494. Submission

3495. Submissive

3496. Submit

3497. Submitted

3498. Subsequent

3499. Subsequently

3500. Substitute

3501. Subtle

3502. Subtract

3503. Subtraction

3504. Succeed

3505. Success

3506. Successful

3507. Succession

3508. Successive

3509. Successor

3510. Sue

Day-118

3511. Sued

3512. Suffer

3513. Suffered

3514. Sufferer

3515. Suffering

3516. Sufficient

3517. Suffix

3518. Suffrage

3519. Sugar

3520. Sugarcane

3521. Suggest

3522. Suggestion

3523. Suggestive

3524. Suing

3525. Suit

3526. Suitability

3527. Suitable

3528. Suite (= a set of connected rooms in a hotel)

3529. Suited

3530. Suitor

3531. Sullen

3532. Sulphur (UK) / Sulfur (USA)

3533. Sulphuric (UK) / Sulfuric (USA)

3534. Sulphurous (UK) / Sulfurous (USA)

3535. Sum

3536. Summary

3537. Summative

3538. Summer

3539. Summit

3540. Sunday

Day-119

3541. Sung

3542. Superintendent

3543. Superior

3544. Superiority

3545. Supervisor

3546. Supper

3547. Supplier

3548. Supplies

3549. Supply

3550. Supplying

3551. Support

3552. Supporter

3553. Supportive

3554. Suppose

3555. Suppress

3556. Suppressive

3557. Suppressor

3558. Sure

3559. Surely

3560. Surge

3561. Surgeon

3562. Surgery

3563. Surplus

3564. Surreal

3565. Surrender

3566. Surround

3567. Survival

3568. Survive

3569. Suspend

3570. Suspense

Day-120

3571. Suspension

3572. Sustain

3573. Sustainability

3574. Sustainable

3575. Swallow

3576. Swam

3577. Swan

3578. Swear

3579. Sweat

3580. Sweep

3581. Sweeper

3582. Sweet

3583. Swell

3584. Swept

3585. Swerve

3586. Swift

3587. Swim

3588. Swimmer

3589. Swimming

3590. Swimming Pool

3591. Swindle

3592. Swindler

3593. Swing

3594. Swollen

3595. Sword

3596. Sworn

3597. Swum

3598. Syllabi

3599. Syllable

3600. Syllabus

Day-121

3601. Symbol

3602. Sympathetic

3603. Sympathy

3604. Symphony

3605. Symposium

3606. Symptom

3607. Symptoms

3608. Synonym

3609. Synonyms

3610. Syntax

3611. Syringe

3612. System

3613. Tab

3614. Table

3615. Tablet

3616. Tabloid

3617. Tacit

3618. Taciturn

3619. Tackle

3620. Tactic

3621. Tactics

3622. Tail

3623. Tale

3624. Talent

3625. Talk

3626. Talkative

3627. Talkies

3628. Talks

3629. Tamarind

3630. Tamper

Day-122

3631. Tangible

3632. Tarzan

3633. Task

3634. Taste

3635. Tasted

3636. Tasty

3637. Tattoo

3638. Tattooist

3639. Taught

3640. Taxation

3641. Taxi

3642. Tea

3643. Teach

3644. Teacher

3645. Teaching

3646. Tear

3647. Tease

3648. Technical

3649. Technically

3650. Technician

3651. Technique

3652. Technology

3653. Tech-savvy

3654. Teen

3655. Teenage

3656. Teenager

3657. Teetotaller (UK) / Teetotaler (USA)

3658. Telecast

3659. Telegram

3660. Telegraph

Day-123

3661. Telepathy

3662. Telephone

3663. Telescope

3664. Television

3665. Teller

3666. Telugu (language)

3667. Temper

3668. Temperature

3669. Temple

3670. Tenant

3671. Tenants

3672. Tender

3673. Tennikoit

3674. Tennis

3675. Tense

3676. Tensed

3677. Tenure

3678. Terminal

3679. Terrible

3680. Terrific

3681. Territory

3682. Terror

3683. Tertiary

3684. Test

3685. Testee

3686. Tester

3687. Testimonials

3688. Testing

3689. Text

3690. Textbook

Day-124

3691. Textile

3692. Texture

3693. Thankful

3694. Theft

3695. Theism

3696. Theist

3697. Theme

3698. Themselves

3699. Theorem

3700. Theorems

3701. Theories

3702. Theorist

3703. Theory

3704. Theses

3705. Thesis

3706. Thief

3707. Thievery

3708. Thieves

3709. Thigh

3710. Thirty

3711. Thoracic

3712. Thorough

3713. Thoroughly

3714. Though

3715. Thought

3716. Thousand

3717. Threat

3718. Threaten

3719. Threshold

3720. Threw

Day-125

3721. Thrice

3722. Thrive

3723. Throat

3724. Throng

3725. Through

3726. Throughout

3727. Throw

3728. Thrown

3729. Thumb

3730. Thunderbolt

3731. Thursday

3732. Thus

3733. Tidal

3734. Tide

3735. Tidy

3736. Tier

3737. Tiger

3738. Time

3739. Timely

3740. Tiny

3741. Tire

3742. Tired

3743. Tiredness

3744. Tobacco

3745. Today

3746. Toddler

3747. Toe

3748. Toes

3749. Toffee

3750. Together

Day-126

3751. Tolerance

3752. Tolerate

3753. Toll

3754. Tomato

3755. Tomatoes

3756. Tomb

3757. Tomorrow

3758. Tone

3759. Tongs

3760. Tongue

3761. Tonight

3762. Torse

3763. Tortoise

3764. Torture

3765. Toss

3766. Toucan

3767. Touch

3768. Tough

3769. Tour

3770. Tourism

3771. Tourist

3772. Tow

3773. Towards

3774. Tower

3775. Trachea

3776. Track

3777. Trade

3778. Trademark

3779. Tradition

3780. Train

Day-127

3781. Trainee

3782. Trainer

3783. Traitor

3784. Tranquil

3785. Tranquillity (UK) / Tranquility (USA)

3786. Transfer

3787. Transferred

3788. Transfers

3789. Transient

3790. Transit

3791. Transition

3792. Translucent

3793. Transmission

3794. Transmit

3795. Transmitted

3796. Transparent

3797. Transplant

3798. Transplantation

3799. Transplanted

3800. Transport

3801. Transported

3802. Transporter

3803. Trap

3804. Trapezium

3805. Trapped

3806. Trauma

3807. Treacherous

3808. Treachery

3809. Tread

3810. Treason

Day-128

3811. Treasure

3812. Treat

3813. Treatment

3814. Treaty

3815. Tree

3816. Tremor

3817. Tremored

3818. Tremors

3819. Trend

3820. Trendies

3821. Trendy

3822. Trespass

3823. Trespasser

3824. Tributaries

3825. Tributary

3826. Tribute

3827. Tributes

3828. Trick

3829. Tricked

3830. Tricky

3831. Tried

3832. Tries

3833. Trigger

3834. Trillion

3835. Trilogy

3836. Trio

3837. Triple

3838. Tripled

3839. Tripod

3840. Triumph

Day-129

3841. Triumphant

3842. Triumphantly

3843. Trivial

3844. Trivialities

3845. Triviality

3846. Trod

3847. Trodden

3848. Troop

3849. Troposphere

3850. Trouble

3851. Trouble shooter

3852. Troublesome

3853. Troupe

3854. Trousers

3855. True

3856. Truly

3857. Trust

3858. Trustee

3859. Try

3860. Tsunami

3861. Tuberculosis

3862. Tuesday

3863. Turkey

3864. Turmeric

3865. Turmoil

3866. Turquoise

3867. Turtle

3868. Tweet

3869. Tweeted

3870. Tweeter

Day-130

3871. Twelfth

3872. Twelve

3873. Twice

3874. Twig

3875. Twilight

3876. Twilit

3877. Twin

3878. Twitch

3879. Twitter

3880. Twittered

3881. Type

3882. Typhoid

3883. Typical

3884. Typist

3885. Ugly

3886. Ultimate

3887. Ultimately

3888. Umbrella

3889. Umpire

3890. Uncle

3891. Unfortunate

3892. Unfortunately

3893. Unique

3894. Universal

3895. Unlawful

3896. Unpleasant

3897. Unravel

3898. Unveil

3899. Upgrade

3900. Upgradation

Day-131

3901. Uranus (planet)

3902. Urban

3903. Urbane (= courteous and refined in manner)

3904. Urgency

3905. Urologist

3906. Urology

3907. Use

3908. Useful

3909. Useless

3910. Usual

3911. Usually

3912. Usurp

3913. Usurper

3914. Utensil

3915. Utility

3916. Vacant

3917. Vacantly

3918. Vacation

3919. Vacuum

3920. Valley

3921. Value

3922. Vanish

3923. Vanished

3924. Vanishingly

3925. Varieties

3926. Variety

3927. Vegetable

3928. Vegetarian

3929. Vegetation

3930. Vehicle

Day-132

3931. Veil

3932. Velocity

3933. Vendor

3934. Ventriloquism

3935. Ventriloquist

3936. Venus (planet)

3937. Verb

3938. Verbal

3939. Verbose

3940. Verdict

3941. Vernacular

3942. Verse

3943. Verses

3944. Versus

3945. Vessel

3946. Veterinary

3947. Vicinity

3948. Vicious

3949. Victim

3950. Video

3951. Vigour (UK) / Vigor (USA)

3952. Village

3953. Vine

3954. Violet

3955. Violin

3956. Violinist

3957. Viral

3958. Virus

3959. Viruses

3960. Visibility

Day-133

3961. Visible

3962. Vision

3963. Visionary

3964. Visual

3965. Visually

3966. Viva voce

3967. Vivid

3968. Vividly

3969. Vlog

3970. Vlogger

3971. Vocal

3972. Vocalist

3973. Vocation

3974. Void

3975. Volcano

3976. Volcanoes

3977. Volleyball

3978. Volume

3979. Voluminous

3980. Voluntarily

3981. Volunteer

3982. Vote

3983. Voter

3984. Voyage

3985. Voyager

3986. Vulnerable

3987. Vulture

3988. Wage

3989. Wait

3990. Waiter

Day-134

3991. Walk

3992. Walker

3993. Wallet

3994. Walrus

3995. Warm

3996. Warranty

3997. Warrior

3998. Washerman

3999. Washerwoman

4000. Wastage

4001. Waste

4002. Watt

4003. Weak

4004. Weakness

4005. Wealth

4006. Wealthy

4007. Wear

4008. Wearable

4009. Weather

4010. Weave

4011. Weaver

4012. Wed

4013. Wedded

4014. Wedding

4015. Wednesday

4016. Week

4017. Weird

4018. Wet

4019. Whale

4020. Wheat

Day-135

4021. Wheel

4022. When

4023. Whenever

4024. Whereas

4025. Wherever

4026. Whether

4027. While

4028. Whilst

4029. Whiskey

4030. Whisper

4031. Whistle

4032. Whole

4033. Wholesale

4034. Wholesaler

4035. Wholly

4036. Whoosh

4037. Wicked

4038. Wicket

4039. Wide

4040. Widespread

4041. Widow

4042. Widower

4043. Width

4044. Wife

4045. Window

4046. Wine

4047. Wire

4048. Withdraw

4049. Withdrawal

4050. Witness

Day-136

4051. Witnesses

4052. Wives

4053. Wolf

4054. Wolves

4055. Womb

4056. Wombs

4057. Wonder

4058. Wonderful

4059. Wooden

4060. Woodpecker

4061. Wool

4062. Woollen (UK) / Woolen (USA)

4063. Work

4064. Worked

4065. Worker

4066. Worm

4067. Worrier

4068. Worries

4069. Worry

4070. Wreck

4071. Wrest (= forcibly pull)

4072. Wrestle

4073. Wrestled

4074. Wrestling

4075. Wrist

4076. Wristwatch

4077. Write

4078. Written

4079. Wrote

4080. Yard

Day-137

4081. Yards

4082. Yawn

4083. Year

4084. Yearn

4085. Yearned

4086. Yen (currency)

4087. Yesterday

4088. Yoga

4089. Yogi

4090. YouTuber

4091. Zeal

4092. Zealous

4093. Zebra

4094. Zigzag

4095. Zinc

4096. Zip

4097. Zoology

4098. Zoom

ABOUT THE AUTHOR

Maruthi Krishna Nivarthi, M.A. (Eng.), (Ph.D.), B.Ed., has been teaching English for the last 15 years. He got the Mandal first rank in his class 7 public exams and the state 21st rank in his B.Ed. entrance exam. In 2017, he qualified APSET. Later, he wrote his Ph.D. Entrance Examination (APRCET) and became the topper of Acharya Nagarjuna University. In addition
to these, he completed a course titled 'Technical English for Engineers conducted by the prestigious IIT, Madras as its national topper receiving ELITE and GOLD category. Regarding publications, he has published a research paper on pronunciation.

In his long career as an English teacher, he taught as a Primary School Teacher, High School Teacher, Head of the Department and Vice-Principal at school level, Lecturer at Intermediate and C.A. levels and Assistant Professor at Engineering level. As a Ph.D. scholar, he has been doing research on spellings for 4 years.